MANAGE YOUR MIND

◆

Set Yourself Free

For Sarah
Christmas 2017
with gratitude for
introducing us to
this old man —
and so much more.

Love, Liz

Love Cuff

MANAGE YOUR MIND

Set Yourself Free

Sidney Rittenberg

ISBN-10 1522860363
ISBN-13 978-1522860365

Cover design by Kathryn Campbell
Printed in the United States of America

Published by East West Insights
www.eastwestinsights.com

CONTENTS

FOREWORD

by Avery Rome

I got to know Sidney Rittenberg because he needed an editor for the book you're reading. Lucky me! Let me introduce him to you. Sidney has already recounted, with cowriter Amanda Bennett, his astonishing autobiography, *The Man Who Stayed Behind.* Years ago he was imprisoned in China, first for six years and then—after reuniting with his family and returning to an active career—for ten years more. The incarcerations were grossly unjust. He wasn't the spy his captors thought they'd captured, yet all that time he was subjected to the horrors of solitary confinement.

Imagine the person you'd be after such torture—angry, scarred, twitchy, bitter. Yet Sidney is none of those things. Instead, he is merry, affectionate, balanced, and fun. He delights in the pleasures and the humor of life, and he has a sense of proportion and joy that draws people to him. At ninety-four he has conceded little to the passage of time.

His mind is sharp and he still wants to do whatever he can to help others, to show them how to use their minds to find greater fulfillment. He sees the big picture, embraces change, and is blessed with a bedrock optimism that accepts reality and still thinks things are going to work out all right.

How does somebody go through what he has endured and come out so together and so strong? How does that happen? No one gets through life without encountering difficulties—illness, depression, pain, loss. Sidney believes that the lessons he has learned can help anyone who is suffering, and in this book, you'll see how you might apply his thoughts and practices to your own problems.

Sidney offers the welcome news that we're stronger than we think. We can learn ways that can guide us through our struggles. We can prevent dark thoughts from sapping our resolve. We can use our minds to deal with negative emotions and help us build on our strengths. We can identify our purpose and find new ways to achieve our goals. We can, says the man who was jailed for so long, find a new freedom that enriches our lives.

—Formerly deputy managing editor of writing & projects at *The Philadelphia Enquirer*, Avery Rome now teaches writing at the University of Pennsylvania.

FOREWORD

by Amanda Bennett

Often, especially during the high-stress, heavy-workload years when Sidney Rittenberg and I were working on the memoir that eventually became *The Man Who Stayed Behind*, I would rail against some heavy burden or another. An unreasonable boss. An unthinking friend. A financial burden. An unfair twist of fate. I would never be happy, or successful, or fulfilled, I thought, unless somehow I managed to twist, torque, and force those circumstances into being the way I wanted them to be.

And then I thought about what Sidney did. It was hard to think of a more unfair fate than being imprisoned for something you didn't do. Hard to imagine a heavier burden than thoughts of your wife and family forcedly separated from you. Hard to think of almost anything in the world harder to endure than solitary confinement. Not for a week. Not for a month. Not for a year, but for two confinements, totaling sixteen long years in all. Nearly half of the life I had lived by the time Sidney and I met.

Somehow, during the second of those two confine-ments, he learned from the horrors of the first. He learned what happened when—during his first imprisonment—he railed against the unfairness of it all. When he tortured himself with self-doubt and recriminations, wondering over and over again what he had done to deserve such a fate. When he drove himself nearly to madness with his thoughts of the world outside, of what he was missing, of the injustice of the situation he found himself in.

The second time he was wiser. Somehow, against all hope, against all reason, against all of our own ideas about what suffering ten years of solitary confinement would bring, he managed to survive. And not only survive but find his own measure of happiness. Alone in a tiny cell, with no company, no comforts, with barely enough to eat, he found a way to unlock his own power. To make it serve him to survive rather than condemn him to madness.

Madness.

It is the one question that almost everyone first asks upon hearing Sidney's remarkable story. Is he mad? Was he driven insane by his torture?

As we worked on the book together, I spent nearly three years with Sidney in almost daily intense meetings, conversation, and exchanged writings. Since then, I have spent another quarter century as his friend and the friend of his extraordinary wife Wang Yulin, and his equally extraordinary four children.

I cannot vouch for the soundness of his sense of humor, which depends to an unseemly degree on hideous puns and wordplay. I cannot explain his continued attachment to the writing style of the British Romantic period (never use a simple word when a complex one will do, and never use one word if there are ten to be had). I cannot explain his eating habits (green vegetables are poison) or the odd quirks of his memory, which always causes him to remember arguments won, and always to forget arguments lost. I can however say one thing for certain: there is no one saner than he.

He made his peace with his horrific circumstances by applying a clear-eyed and realistic view of his situation and then rigorously governing his mind and his actions accordingly. He looked at the four walls of his cell. He analyzed the circumstances that had put him there. Most extraordinarily, he made a wrenching acknowledgement that mental self-torture would do nothing to protect his family outside, and then schooled himself away from such thoughts. Instead, he evaluated exactly what his present situation entailed—four walls, a bed, his mind, and his will—and set about making the most of those assets while refusing to succumb as he had the first time around to painful and fruitless battering against circumstances he could in no way change.

Thus over ten years, although others set the conditions of his days, he was the master of his own life. He ordered his own thoughts. He exercised. When allowed books, he studied. When his exemplary conduct won him a few moments of chat with guards who admired him in spite of themselves, he spoke to them as human beings and not captors. He never gave up hope that one day he would be released, but never wallowed in the thought that he might not.

How, then, could I—or anyone—feel oppressed by the comparatively weak prisons of circumstance that confine us? Why not learn voluntarily to do what Sidney was forced to learn? Take a realistic view of our circumstances. Understand what is changeable and what is permanent. Take advantage of the amazing range of human endeavor that is possible even within the most constrained circumstances.

Some people say that only an extraordinary person could do what Sidney did. I admit he really is extraordinary. But few of us will face solitary. All of us face limitations in our lives. Sidney says there is nothing extraordinary in what he did or thought. He believes everyone can do it. He wrote this book to show us how.

—After twenty-three years as a reporter with the
Wall Street Journal, Amanda Bennett worked as managing
editor at *The Oregonian*, editor of the *Philadelphia Enquirer*,
and executive editor at *Bloomberg News*.
She has written six nonfiction books.

ACKNOWLEDGMENTS

For nearly four decades, I have been carrying these experiences around with me like a hen with an egg that has to be laid. Finally, for better or for worse, I have laid the egg. (I know, not really a happy metaphor.)

This was only possible because of the unfailing encouragement, support, and advice from my wife/sweetheart/partner/chief critic, Yulin Wang Rittenberg.

That this little book appears in its present presentable shape is due to the talented editing and wise guidance of Avery Rome, to whom I am deeply indebted.

I was fortunate to have the expert facilitation of editor Meredith Bailey and cover designer Kathy Campbell.

Other volunteer readers who provided feedback include Wendy Samberg, Ping and Shirley Kiang, Joan Goldsmith, and Ken Cloke. Many thanks to all these good friends.

Special thanks to our psychologist friend, Dr Barry Goodfield, who offered valuable support and feedback.

Special appreciation goes to accomplished author Dori Jones Yang who volunteered to make all the preparations for editing, designing, and publishing this book.

And thanks in advance to the readers from whom I hope to hear.

INTRODUCTION

My life experiences have taught me the freedom-giving powers of human reason. With this gift, we need not be driven blindly by negative emotions, conscious or unconscious. We can avoid being thrown by sudden shocks or overwhelmed by grief. We can set rational goals and move, through trial and error, toward their fulfillment.

This understanding came to me in the course of sixteen years of wrongful solitary confinement in Chinese prisons. They taught me that *we are much stronger than we think*. To take the initiative and realize our full strength, we need only learn to manage our minds.

Let me now, at age ninety-four, show you how I learned to do this. I did it, not because I was particularly smart or tough, but simply because *I had to*. I was not going to let wrongful imprisonment ruin my life.

Dear Reader, please pay attention to this caveat: I am not suggesting that my experience with management of mind can lead to a kind of euphoric nirvana where all ills are cured and all issues resolved. What I am saying is that I believe you can, through enlightened self-training, gain a great deal of control over your moods and emotions. You can win a large measure of the initiative over your own mind and thereby enjoy a new sense of freedom, stability, and happiness.

One

....

The Shock

I am cut to th' brains.
—William Shakespeare, *King Lear*

"How does a good Jewish boy from Charleston, South Carolina, end up in a Chinese prison?"

Good question. It was raised by an American university professor at a lecture I gave shortly after my release from prison in November 1977. I told the professor that during World War II the U.S. Army had trained me in Chinese and in September 1945 sent me to China. After my honorable discharge four months later, I joined the United Nations famine relief effort in China.

During my first few years there, I managed to find underground workers of the Chinese Communist Party. Coming from a radical civil rights and labor background in the American South, I was inspired by their heroic

1

battle for land, peace, and democracy against what Theodore White called the "incestuous" dictatorship of Chiang Kai-shek.

It bothered me that the real power in our aging American democracy was being monopolized by big money—those whom we Southerners called the "Big Mules." From the young Chinese revolutionaries I embraced the vision of a genuine sort of popular town-hall democracy in which, as revolutionary forerunner Sun Yat-sen had envisioned, "each tiller would have the tiller's own land," and capital would be regulated for the public good. I decided to stay behind in China to support their struggle.

I worked for thirty-odd (really odd!) years for the new Communist-led society, training journalists working in English, translating major Party documents and the writings of Mao Zedong, in addition to writing, editing, and sometimes broadcasting the news. What took place in China was not what I, or anyone else, had expected. Still, while many intellectuals suffered, the positive changes in most people's lives were tremendous and I never lost faith in the revolution.

Not even during my sixteen years in solitary, under suspicion of being an American spy. There was no trial. No one presented evidence. There were no witnesses. Just isolation, grilling, and suspicion.

Readers who want more details on my case are referred to my book, *The Man Who Stayed Behind*, coauthored with Amanda Bennett. I will not retell that story here, but let me just say that I was imprisoned in two different stretches: from February 1949 to April 1955 and from February 1968 to November 1977.

As my American journalist friend, the late Al Ravenholt, pointed out, each time I was thrown into solitary by "an old man"—first, Stalin, and then Mao—and each time I was released by their deaths. Had they been younger, I might still be locked up.

Two

....

The Crash

This fellow is dancing mad!
He hath been bitten by the Tarantula.
— Edgar Allen Poe, "The Gold Bug"

Poe was wrong—while the great hairy tarantula may make fruit traders angry, it does not make men mad. But when reality becomes too painful to bear, the merciful mind turns the switch that shuts it out. After the first shattering shock, my unexpected arrest at the very height of elation when the Communists were on the verge of victory in 1949—and after a later series of shocks, frustrations, and disappointments while imprisoned—my mind threw the switch, and I went mad.

The final blow came after the interrogator had, in his first show of kindness, promised to help me whenever I felt the need to talk with someone. At the same time, my jailors began giving me two little white pills, three times a day.

"You're catching the flu," they said. "Take these."

"I'm not catching the flu."

"Well, you're going to take them anyway!"

The pills were probably some sort of amphetamine. I noticed they increased my nervous tension and made it hard to sleep. Worse were the nights: I would fall asleep and then startle awake.

After several episodes of this, I suddenly awoke one night with a feeling of blind terror. Believing in the promise of help, I pleaded with the guard to send for the interrogator. "I need help, now!" I begged, in a panic.

When the interrogator arrived, he unlocked the door and dangled a pair of manacles at me. "If you don't quiet down, and if you continue to violate discipline, we will have to discipline you!" he snarled. Then he slammed the door and disappeared.

Feeling hurt and betrayed, I agonized through the night, watching the tiny flame from the bean-oil wick in a little saucer on a ledge on the wall. The flicker of that flame in that dark cell began to grow on me. It took the form of a little dancing figure who seemed to be reaching out to me; it had something to say. But what?

The next morning in the interrogation chamber, the interrogator smiled pleasantly at me and asked, "What was all the fuss about?"

"I was upset, and you promised to help me," I replied.

At this point, one of the guards appeared with a *mantou* (steamed bread roll), saying, "You're probably hungry. Eat this."

I took a couple of bites, thinking about *Alice's Adventures in Wonderland*, how Alice ate the little cakes to change her size. *Something's going to happen to me,* I thought as I hungrily wolfed down the mantou. Sure enough, after a couple of bites, I keeled over sideways and fell on the floor, out like a light. When I woke up, three guards were carrying me back to my cell while I laughed hysterically and tried to break free. They put me down on the *kang* (brick oven-bed) and, to quiet me down, they took my overcoat and held it down over my face. I was suffocating. I struggled and struggled, in vain.

That was my last sane moment for months to come.

♦

For who knows how long after that, I lived in a horrible nightmare filled with hysteria, hallucinations, mortal fears, ravings, and compulsions like chewing and swallowing anything in sight. Sometimes I was clamped into tight manacles till I fainted. I'd wake up to find my wrists bleeding as I was taunted and spurned by the guards.

It was perhaps six months before I began making my way out of the madness and back to a quiet sanity. The prison staff also began to help me recover. They clearly knew what was going on—they had seen it many times before. They would give me little tasks to perform—like washing my handkerchief or underwear—and coach me through the process, so that I began slowly to regain some confidence in myself. They also brought in a new team of friendly, kindly—but still very reserved—guards to change the atmosphere. I saw smiles for the first time in, it seemed, ages.

That episode of madness was important because in its wake it left the frequent panic attacks that plagued me for twenty years—the elimination of which was a decisive step in my learning how to manage my mind.

Our real story begins here.

Three

....

Learning to Manage Your Mind

"This man invented cognitive therapy,
all by himself."

—Dr. Aaron Kaplan, Professor of Psychiatry,
speaking about Sidney Rittenberg after a talk he gave
on his experiences in solitary

Now I will try to explain how I learned to manage my mind
to meet the challenges of long-term solitary confinement,
how this led to a much happier, more stable, and more
fulfilling life later on, and how you can learn to manage
your mind.

My experience has convinced me that all of us—this
includes *you*—tend to underestimate our own inner
strength. Much of the alarmist messaging expressed in
the media, advertising, and movies, makes us feel doubt-
ful and insecure: *You're in danger! You're weak! You can't*

make it! Life is tough, and then you die! So take this pill. Buy that. Travel there. Run, run, run! Get away! Hunker down! Escape!

Instead of giving in to fear and anxiety, tune into yourself. We have untapped inner resources that we can draw on, develop, expand, depend on. I know this through personal experience, and I have seen many other people find new courage and confidence within themselves. Life can be a marvelous adventure, full of joy and learning—your life can make a lasting difference. What better reason could I have for writing this for you, at age ninety-four?

I learned that the key to a fulfilling life is to (a) clarify your purpose; (b) find effective methods to attain that purpose; and (c) train your will to focus on following that method to success. There are two processes necessary to fulfilling your purpose: one is called Truth and the other, Progress.

Truth

Many different trains of thought pass through our minds at any given moment. Some provide a more or less clear, accurate picture of what is going on, and how it relates to our own best interests. Others are murky, inaccurate, illusory, distorted by bias or presupposition. We find the truth by learning to distinguish between these two kinds of ideas, separating the sheep from the goats, if you will—embracing reality and dispelling illusion. Remember that such clarity requires a constant effort. But we are rewarded by the delight of discovery: as scientists know, one of the greatest human joys is the discovery of a truth.

This fact struck me, full force, as a sophomore at Chapel Hill, when I read Kant's *Critique of Pure Reason*. I thrilled at the power of the human mind to reach the truth through analysis of facts and synthesis of conclusions.

Progress

When your strengths prevail over your weaknesses, you make headway. If you have a clear perception of your strengths and weaknesses—and if you are able to deploy your strengths to deal with your weaknesses—then you move forward. Actually, there is no other path to progress. All the teaching, guidance, reading, and other outside influences have a fundamental effect on us only insofar as they help us use our strengths to overcome our weaknesses. That is the process that decides whether we go forward or backward.

During the mental purgatory that is solitary confinement, I had to assess my strengths and my weaknesses as well as the favorable and unfavorable circumstances under which I had to struggle.

These were my strengths, as I saw them.

My purpose was clear and consistent: to make my life a contribution to the freedom, happiness, and progress of the human race. I was determined to pursue this purpose and uphold my belief in the importance of New China to human civilization. I would stick to the truth. I detested the idea of betraying my ideals or giving up, in any form.

I had received a good education; I had been trained in logic and in scientific thinking. I had learned some psychology. I had memorized lots of good literature and poetry. And I had known wonderful, inspiring human beings, both in America and in China. Remembering their goodness and courage set an example for me and gave me strength.

I had been trained in the Southern movement for workers' rights, for equality, for democracy not controlled by money. I had some experience in struggling against great odds.

I knew something about how to project the image of who I was to the Chinese, and I was perfectly fluent in the language.

I had a highly developed capacity for love, for people, and for my wonderful wife and children—although I might never see them again.

These were my weaknesses, as I saw them:

I was not physically courageous. I was afraid of pain and of death.

I was cut off from any opportunity to appeal my case, to confront evidence or witnesses, to express myself to my captors. Even during the interrogations, I was not allowed to speak on my own behalf—only to answer questions.

I had been through one terrifying mental breakdown in prison, and I was very much afraid of having another.

So how was I to mobilize my strengths against my weaknesses, and thus deal successfully with this crisis? Some things were clear. I had to use my clarity of purpose and my stubborn determination to pursue my ideals to handle my lack of physical courage and the long period of testing with no clear outcome.

I had to use my understanding of China and my experience in close harmony with the Chinese people to win their empathy by the way I conducted myself in prison. I knew what values they held dear and what traits they admired, and I shared most of them.

I had to draw on my education and experience, particularly

my training in logic and the theory of knowledge, to learn how to lead a meaningful life, all by myself, in solitary.

I had to maintain and improve my health, physical and mental, and to draw on my store of poetry, literature, and even fairy tales, to keep up my morale and my level of activity.

I understood that the key point was to lead my life in that little cell, and relate to the prison personnel, in such a way that I could consistently express who I was and what I believed. The peephole in the door played a prominent role in my new thinking. At first, I hated the peephole. The guard watched me 24-7, with the help of a second peephole by the commode. He looked in, but I was not allowed to look out. Solitude without privacy, I called it.

Then I realized the power in the Chinese philosophical saying: Turn a bad thing into a good thing, and watch out that a good thing doesn't turn into a bad one (by going to extremes).

I realized that the annoying peephole, like everything else, had another side. It was my only channel of contact with the authorities. The guard and the keepers had to observe whatever I showed them. If what they saw was a studious man who respected the territory and kept it clean, who didn't waste food, who obeyed the prison rules, who was quiet and orderly, who clearly was following a set of ideals, they would draw their own conclusions about whether this person was an enemy or not.

Diligent study of books important to the Chinese people was another way to arouse some empathy from those managing me from day to day. Sooner or later, a first-hand understanding of who I really was would surely get through. And it did, since these changes resulted in much better treatment for me, even though my behavior alone couldn't settle my case.

I don't look back on my prison studies with regret. In spite of the terrible isolation, my time spent studying there was an *addition* to my life, rather than a subtraction. Some fundamental facts of life were burned into me by my struggles to overcome isolation and wrong. I learned something (still learning today!) about what is vitally important in life. What is it that you really can't live without? For me, this became clear.

The first is love. Love for the people, because that leads to dedication and thankfulness. Without dedication there's no firm purpose, while without thankfulness there's no happiness. Also, love for learning, because without learning there's no real freedom. And, emphatically, love for my soul-mate, Yulin, and our children, because they are a vital part of me.

The second is confidence in my own ability to stand up to severe challenges and make my way through them.

The third is the process described above, of assessing my own strengths and weaknesses and moving forward in life by pitting the strengths against the weaknesses.

Perhaps one of the most surprising strengths I called upon—during the most trying times in fact—was my knowledge of children's stories and fairy tales. These stories were deeply ingrained in my consciousness and didn't require my higher thought centers to function very well. When I was going through severe "third-degree" interrogation—nine furious people shouting at me for long hours, sometimes surrounding me with fists raised (they never hit me), or banging on the door to keep me from sleeping at night (I slept anyway)—and my mind was fatigued and dull, two stories in particular sustained me.

One was that tale of *The Little Engine That Could*. Like the intrepid train, I would tell myself, *Well, I'm still here, so if it doesn't get any worse than this, I can take it*. In my mind's eye, I could see the intrepid little engine chugging its way uphill, saying "I think I can, I think it can, I think I can . . ."

Another fairy tale that helped me keep a clear head under serious stress was more complicated. It takes a while to tell.

There was a very selfish and very spoiled little boy who had all sorts of toys and sweetmeats and beautiful clothes, but he couldn't stand sharing his goodies with other children. One day, his fairy godmother appeared and told him she would grant him one wish. His wish was to have all the wonderful toys, eats, and clothes that his heart desired, but in a place where other kids couldn't even see them.

With a wave of the fairy godmother's wand, his wish was granted. He found himself in a magnificent palace, heaped with delicious cakes and candies, beautiful clothing, and toys galore.

The palace was not like other buildings—the walls consisted of half windows and half mirrors, one window, one mirror, from end to end, on and on. But the boy paid no attention to this.

He put on the magnificent clothing, preened before the mirrors, stuffed himself with delicious food, and began playing with his wonderful toys.

"At last," he exclaimed, "I have everything I want and those other kids can't even see what I have!"

As he spoke, there was a hollow rumbling sound and all the mirrors got wider, as the windows got narrower.

"Who cares?" said the little boy. "I don't need to see out, and I don't want them to see in!"

Again, a hollow rumbling sound, and the windows narrowed to a tiny crack as the mirrors covered almost all of the walls. But the little boy enjoyed showing off his new clothes in the bigger mirrors even more as he munched delectable cakes and candies.

"See if I care," he said, stretching out on the soft, fragrant bed to sleep.

Two days passed and the almost windowless palace began to pall. The little boy tried to see out into the garden, but the windows were too narrow— he could see nothing. Gradually, he got tired of dressing up and admiring himself in the huge mirrors. He began to mope, wondering why, when he had everything he had ever wanted, he was so sad.

One morning he woke up to find a little bird with a broken wing, hopping forlornly around his bedroom and then perching on a beam under the ceiling. The little boy began to have a strange new emotion. "I know just how you must feel," he said. "I'm going to make a splint for your broken wing." He broke off a wooden panel from a toy boat and a piece from the curtain to hold it on. As he did, he heard the sound of harps and oboes—and the windows opened a little bit, as the mirrors began to shrink.

The bird was high up, so the little boy pulled over a big table and placed a smaller table and a chair on top of it, so he could reach the bird. Again, harps and oboes, and the windows opened another crack. At last the boy reached the bird and tied the splint to its wing. Then he carried the bird over to a window and said, "I can't get out of here and go home—the window's too small. But at least I can set you free."

He thrust the bird through the window to freedom, and as he did so there was a great crescendo of triumphant music. The windows opened wide, and the little boy himself was free.

How happy he was! And when he got home, the first thing he said was "Mom, let's invite the other kids to a big party. I want to share everything I have with them."

I loved this story and drew sustenance from it in the hardest of times. To me, it demonstrated such a simple, powerful truth, one contained in the Bible: It *is* better to give than to receive. When we give, we open our hearts so that we can receive, whereas if we focus on taking, our hearts tend to close to protect what we have taken. When

I told myself this story, I thrilled at the liberating power of love.

But where did this story come from? Years later, after I had been freed from prison and had returned to the United States, I went to the New York Public Library to consult their experts on fairy tales from all over the world. I asked them to trace the story for me, because I couldn't remember where I got it.

After much research, they told me that parts of the story were reminiscent of some European tales, but actually it seemed I had made it up in its present form. My faith in the healing power of unselfish love and my suffering from the distortion created by narrow selfishness fashioned itself into this story, which, in turn, pointed the way for me to behave. Whatever the circumstances, keep doing whatever you can to make a better world. It takes you out of yourself and into the vibrancy of life.

Even when we're out of childhood, we can pay attention to the morals and the good sense we learn from poetry, fairy tales, Bible stories, and so on. They are always there when we need them, and we need to keep them close by. If commercialism and vulgar pursuits push them out of our consciousness, we will lose an invaluable part of our education.

Taking stock of my strengths and harnessing them to overcome my weaknesses had another added benefit. It helped me to remember that the arrow of time moves ever forward. Nature evolves. Society grows in enlightenment. Progress is the norm. Progress for human beings requires much learning and subjective effort. I knew that this principle applied anywhere, to anyone—including to me in solitary.

Four

....

Twelve Key Lessons, Learned the Hard Way

"I have been studying how I may compare
this prison where I live unto the world:
And for because the world is populous
And here is not a creature but myself,
I cannot do it: yet I'll hammer it out."

—Shakespeare, *Richard II*

Here are twelve personal lessons,
describing what I discovered,
through trial and error, about using my
strengths against my weaknesses
and learning to manage my mind.

Lesson 1

DON'T COVER UP PROBLEMS

When the warden advised me to forget the harsh treatment, I immediately made up my mind to do no such thing. I didn't want to hide the painful experiences so that, like a splinter that the skin grows over, they might hurt later on when I had forgotten about the source of the pain. The rule I lived by was this: don't obsess over painful experiences, but keep them in consciousness so that you can gradually understand them and remove the pain.

It worked. Today, looking back at the misery of solitary, I have no pain whatsoever.

I think it's best if people with painful or frightening events in their past learn to gradually face them, get used to them, eliminate the fear or anger they inspire, and thus overcome and eliminate their impact.

Lesson 2

CELEBRATE THE IMPROVEMENTS

I learned that no matter how bad things looked, I always needed to put my best foot forward. As the weeks turned into months and then years, and time seemed to deepen my isolation, I paid attention every day to the aspects in which I was improving, how I was better than last year or better than last month. For example, I noted when I became less wobbly on my feet, when I started sleeping better, and when my Chinese writing began to improve. One day I discovered that steeping steamed cornbread in thin cabbage soup made it quite tasty. So, I was getting better, at least in some ways. Stressing areas of progress gives one badly needed encouragement and hope. Nobody else was cheering me on, so I had to do it myself.

Lesson 3

DRAW ON CULTURE

The reams of poetry and stories I had learned by heart were an endless source of support. An outstanding example of this was a verse I had memorized in college from Percy Bysshe Shelley's "Prometheus Unbound." It seemed tailor-made for my situation.

> *To suffer woes which Hope thinks infinite;*
> *To forgive wrongs darker than death or night;*
> *To defy Power, which seems omnipotent;*
>
> *To love, and bear; to hope till Hope creates*
>
> *From its own wreck the thing it contemplates;*
> *Neither to change, nor falter, nor repent;*
> *This, like thy glory, Titan, is to be*
> *Good, great and joyous, beautiful and free;*
> *This is alone Life, Joy, Empire and Victory.*

This was written for me, I thought. I repeated and exulted in the line, "Neither to change, nor falter, nor repent."

My old friend Deng Tuo, once in charge of the *People's*

Daily, the official Communist Party newspaper, was among the first victims of the Cultural Revolution. With an extremely weak heart, he relied on medication to keep going. Deng worked for fair play and democracy within the Party, which is why he came under vicious attack by the strict advocates of "total dictatorship." Knowing that his heart could not withstand the cruel struggles that faced him, and with the reluctant consent of his loving and also persecuted wife, he stopped his medication and departed gracefully from this world.

I drew powerful support from a quatrain Deng Tuo penned before he died:

> *With truth in my heart,*
> *And a pen in my hand;*
> *Selfless and fearless,*
> *I am a free man.*

My friend's words sank deep into my heart. If I could rid myself of the fear of death and hardship, and if I could place my own misfortune within the broad context of China's rise from poverty and ignorance, then I would be free from fear and narrow selfishness.

Indeed, why fear death? I reasoned. It is a quietude, without pain, regret, or remorse. The certainty of death, moreover, is what makes life so precious. I would fight for an extended life, to leave behind more of a contribution to my fellow humans, but once death came it would not hurt. Only the fear of death hurts—and detracts from our joy in living. Deng Tuo was right: a person who can break through the confines of a narrow egotism and dedicate himself or herself to a noble cause may be unafraid of death or hardship and could indeed be free.

Regardless of my incarceration, that possibility was open to me.

I thought a lot about my experience with fear. All my life, I had been afraid of this and that—of polio as a child, of bullies at school, of pole climbing in the Army, of bombing raids in China. What had fear gotten me? Being afraid had not prevented me from being forced to endure long years of solitary imprisonment. Fear didn't help. It was useless.

Get rid of it! I thought. And I worked, constantly, toward that goal.

I meditated on Deng Tuo's lines from time to time, and when I did I could feel a relaxation in the taut muscles in my shoulders, neck, and back; a deep feeling of peace came into my heart.

I had never trained in meditation. Even so, my

unskilled practice would bring me relaxation and peace of mind. Simply being conscious of my anxieties, my "wishes and suspicions," didn't solve any problems. It did, however, make the issues clear and often lead to an unraveling and a resolution.

Traditional Chinese medicine holds that wherever there is pain, something is closed that should be open. Open it, and you banish the pain. I think this principle applies especially to mental discomfort.

Lesson 4

PLAN YOUR DAY

As the ancients put it, by taking thought alone we cannot add a cubit to our stature. I had to work out an active program every day to brace myself against the crushing loneliness. For example, I had a "comic hour" on most days (along with the study hours I set, cleanup time, exercises, etc.) during which I would think up the comical aspects of my situation and hold imaginary outrageous talks with the keepers and interrogators.

Once, I prepared this little speech for my next grilling: "Look, I respect your system of justice, but I must tell you that I am not temperamentally suited to this sort of life in solitary. I am a very gregarious person, rather talkative, and I like being around people. So, if you don't mind, I'd like to ask for a transfer to the Beijing Municipal Prison that we foreigners are taken to visit—the one where the inmates had their own study groups, and where they were busy painting murals on the walls, kneading dough for Chinese dumplings, writing and reciting poetry…"

The thought of my jailers' faces if I said any such thing

was hilarious.

Another weird example of comic relief. A highly objectionable man in the cell next to mine would curse the young country boy on guard duty in an extremely contemptuous way. The guards had no keys to the cell, and no way to deal with such personal attacks. I resented the abuse and thought it was unfair. But what could I do?

It turned out there was something. The man's commode and washbasin shared the same water supply as mine—they were on opposite sides of the same cell wall. One day, when I heard his water running in the basin, I flushed my toilet and turned my basin water on, full force. That cut his water down to a thin flow, which caused him to turn his faucet on as far as it could go. When I heard his water running, I immediately shut mine off, so that the water in his basin surged forth suddenly and splashed all over him. I could hear him stamping around and cursing, so I knew he had been punished. How good I felt about that!

Lesson 5

BE CAREFUL
OF THE STORIES
YOU TELL YOURSELF

Find the "triggers" that cause negative mood swings and eliminate them.

One day, after some time in isolation, a terrible thought struck me: Even if I ever got out, I would never be a normal person again. I didn't know how to talk to people, how to listen, how to move about in society. I was only fit to be alone!

Wham! I sank.

But thinking it over, a different idea popped up. *Wait a minute—when did you start feeling so depressed?* said a voice in the back of my head. *Was it when they first locked you up? No, it hit you when you told yourself this story, "I can't be normal." It's your own story that got you down, not the reality.*

Poof! The depression was gone, as quickly as it had come.

I realized that sanity and survival depend on keeping a clear head, and that I needed to beware of the stories I was telling myself—not confuse them with reality. When you have a mood swing, analyze what triggered it. Often, it's not what you might think. Expose the trigger, and you solve the problem.

Although many different thoughts compete for our attention at any given moment, usually one way of thinking represents our better judgment. I call it "the little voice." If we can pay attention and listen to it, it may show us the way.

Lesson 6

STICK TO YOUR PURPOSE

In March 1980, I moved back to the States, to continue working on bridging U.S-China relations from this side of the Pacific. I was warmly welcomed by both media and government—even formally received by Richard Holbrook, Assistant Secretary of State for Asia. I was interviewed by *The New York Times*, in a piece covering the entire second page, and did five specials with Mike Wallace (later a good friend) on "60 Minutes," which set a new record for number of interviews on that program. I became Professor of China Studies at the New School in New York, then, from 1994, became Frey Distinguished Professor of Chinese History at my Alma Mater, University of North Carolina at Chapel Hill. Finally, after we settled in the Seattle Area (closer to China for our repeated return flights), I became Visiting Professor of China Studies and Senior Advisor at Pacific Lutheran University.

At that school, in 1997, I was asked to teach a course in Chinese Culture and Thought. Every year, I would ask my class three questions. The first question is: "How would you go about choosing a new car?" The answers pour out enthusiastically: "Talk to friends about their experiences." "Read some of the car literature." "Test-drive different models." Then I ask the second and third questions: "What picture do you have in your head of yourself as a happy and successful person twenty years from now?" and "What do happiness and success look like to you?" Dead silence every time.

Then I say, "You will probably own dozens of cars, but you only have one life. Why is it that you pay more attention to selecting a car than you do to picking the best possible life for yourself?"

Then some bold young person takes a shot at it. "I think of happiness as an ideal wife and kids, nice house, good job, enough of everything we need."

Then I say, "Is that enough? What's the difference between your idea and the way a well-fed, much-loved puppy feels, stretched out in front of the fireplace while master and mistress sit there watching TV?"

Finally, usually in a day or two, the students will begin saying things like, "Of course I want to live in freedom, have my privacy, and make a difference with my life . . . "

After several sessions, the class puts together some concepts of distinctively human (not canine) happiness that begin to make sense. But this process reveals a major problem: How can your life be fulfilling, if you don't have a clear and uplifting purpose to fulfill? Purpose tells you the real substance of a person, his or her essence. It's what makes you similar to or different from anyone or anything else, what explains your role in life. Purpose shows why you are as you are, and where you are headed. If you ask people about their life purpose, they may not tell you the truth. One, because they are unable to state it clearly, and two, because they may want to conceal it. "By their fruits ye shall know them," the Bible says.

So look at the roles these people have played in the past, and where they are today, and that span gives you the trajectory, pointing toward their futures. It reveals their true aims, whether or not they are fully conscious of them. It's important to know that everyone does have a purpose, but not everyone is conscious of it. To take the initiative in your life, that consciousness is essential.

Of course, purpose, like anything else, may change. Consider Zeno's paradoxes. The ancient Greek sage, Zeno, argued that motion was impossible—a man moving toward a door must cover half the distance first, and half of the remaining distance, then half of the new remainder, and so on ad infinitum. In theory, he can never actually arrive at the door, because he can never finish crossing those diminishing halves. Of course, we know this is not true, but how can we refute Zeno's dilemma? (The ancient Chinese have almost exactly the same paradoxes, but they used them to prove the opposite point—that everything is always in motion.)

The refutation of Zeno is easy. It has to do with the nature of movement. Every entity is constantly in motion, and motion consists of the entity being where it is at the moment, but also partly where it is coming from, and partly where it is going. That's what motion actually implies. It embodies past, present, and future. It is defined by change. One's life purpose must use the opportunities that the possibility of change offers to move forward.

So because, despite Zeno, everything changes, a set life purpose can change as well. Some students set their minds to make lots of money so they can use it to help people, to do some good in the world. But the process of making money exerts its own influence. Many of those who pursue it may gradually lose their innocence and decide, instead, just to increase their own wealth and power and to use philanthropy mainly to cover their tracks. They don't change overnight—they are blindsided by gradual change, a slow leaning, and they often don't realize that it's happening. That's also why some movements that try to create an ideal society change in the process of managing power and end up as repressive as the tyrants they overthrew.

A clear purpose can be a powerful engine that drives you forward, that is always there for you, no matter how trying the circumstances. The purpose and the method *interpenetrate*: the method embodies the purpose. As Gandhi pointed out: "Be the change you wish to see in the world." You express your purpose by the method you use to achieve it. And since method and process—and change—are the true tangibles we have, purpose gives meaning to what you do.

As a boy, I accepted the idea that the real meaning in human life lay in what one can give to the freedom and happiness of others. Making a contribution was the stable, dependable source of human well-being.

Thrown into solitary confinement, I made up my mind to find all possible ways, even if they were infinitesimal, to do some good in the world. I told myself that, as an American, I was born with the right to "life, liberty, and the pursuit of happiness," and, as long as I was alive, no one could ever take those rights completely away from me—as long as I didn't give them up!

So I decided to do little things like keeping the cell

squeaky clean, from the floor to as high up as I could reach on the walls. I made sure that every grain of food ended up in my mouth, even if it had fallen on the floor. I took advantage of the rare opportunities to chat for a minute with a curious guard, who would talk to me when no other guards were in the corridor. I'd share a little story about America, something I thought he could relate to.

Any of these accomplishments, however tiny, gave me a sense of progress in my life. I often thought of those lines from Portia in Shakespeare's *Merchant of Venice:* "How far that little candle throws its beams! So shines a good deed in a naughty world."

But one day I suffered doubts. *Everything I can do here is infinitesimal and unimportant, plus no one will ever even know about it. What's the use?* Then, better judgment spoke up. *Einstein made enormous contributions, but ten thousand years from now how big will Einstein look? It is not about the scale of what you do, it's about the quality— your purpose! Human life itself is valued in terms of quality, not quantity. It's about whether you contributed at all, not about how much.*

In a sense, I felt that my daily study was a contribution, because it was intended to make me better able to serve in the future. It had meaning. I thought about the poem "A

Psalm of Life" by Henry Wadsworth Longfellow—a poem that held special meaning for both my father and me:

Life is real! Life is earnest!
And the grave is not the goal;
Dust thou art, to dust returnest,
Was not spoken of the soul.

I was deeply persuaded that as long as we could add even one drop to the long river of human progress, that drop would go on and on, regardless of whether we were conscious of it, wave upon wave, till the end of time. In that drop lies our true immortality.

Lesson 7

LINK MIND AND HEART

When we set ourselves a purpose, we need both clear thinking and powerful emotional drive. Negative emotions will disrupt and frustrate our advancement. But we cannot proceed without emotion, because thinking and emoting are hardwired together in our brains.

The problem is that powerful negative emotions can't be controlled simply by preaching at them, by giving them rational arguments. What works is to generate still more powerful positive emotions to overwhelm the negative ones. Creating positive emotions still requires the use of reasoning, but the contest takes place within the realm of emotion.

Why did I crash during my first year in prison? While I could understand what was going on intellectually, and even justify it, I could not deal with the powerful feelings of hurt and frustration, the agony of being misunderstood.

Even after my imprisonment ended, I continued to learn how to deal with negative emotions. I had begun learning how to deal with negative emotions before my arrest, but I had done this only on a small scale. For example,

I knew that eating fatty pork would make me gain weight and lead to cardiovascular problems, but I had a weakness for a delectable Hunanese dish of red-braised pork. The way I killed this craving was to imagine myself as grossly obese with a weak heart. That turned the desire into disgust, and I was free.

An impressive example occurred during the Tangshan Earthquake of 1976. Hundreds of thousands perished in this great temblor, and Qincheng Prison, where I was incarcerated, shook violently. The prisoners were all moved, one by one, to emergency pup tents that had been erected in the prison courtyard. Now, instead of one guard watching a dozen cells, one guard monitored each individual tent, and the tents were so far apart that the guard could talk with the prisoner without attracting an officer's attention. This was a great break for me—what I needed most in the world was someone to talk to.

When a new guard came on the evening shift, he told me that another even larger quake was expected that night, and that the center would be right there at our prison. My tent was right next to a three-story cellblock. It could fall on me! I tossed and turned all night until the young guard said, "What's the matter with you? Why aren't you sleeping?"

"How can I sleep," I told him, "when this building may fall on me any minute now?"

This young country boy in uniform drew himself up to his full height, and said, "Look, my duty is to protect your life. You see me—I'm standing here between you and the building. If anyone gets killed, I'll be the first to die—and I'm not afraid. I'm doing my duty. Now, you do your duty and go to sleep! I'm watching over you!"

I looked at this slip of a Chinese lad, taking on more than his share of the danger to protect a foreigner who, as far as he knew, was his enemy. What kind of morality was he showing, compared to my cringing and whining? Filled with these powerful new emotions, I felt the fear vanish, and I slept easily until the next morning.

I realized that whenever I felt blocked by negative emotions, I had to generate powerful positive emotions to overcome them. From this viewpoint, I understood one reason for my failures in the past.

Back in my college Psychology 101 class, I had learned that one of the most powerful impressions on the brain comes from the sound of your own voice. I remembered that in solitary—whenever I was assailed by doubts or fears, and I felt the onset of that distinctive pall that signals approaching depression, I would immediately tell myself, *I know this feeling. I know what you're up to—you're trying to upset me. No way! Get away from here!* And it would slink away immediately, tail between its legs.

Lesson 8

ROOT OUT BIAS
FROM YOUR JUDGMENTS

I had to learn to adopt an objective standpoint, consistent with my purpose, to distinguish the true from the false. For example, one day the interrogators told me, over and over, that no matter whether I confessed or not, I would never, ever get out of this prison.

"Confess, and you will get better living conditions. You will be allowed to take part in group study and have wider freedom—but you will never leave this prison!"

In bed that night, I struggled. *If I'm going to be locked up all my life*, I thought, *what's the point in living?* Instinctively, though, I rejected hopelessness and the voice of better judgment spoke up in the back of my head. *Wait a minute*, it said. *You're supposed to be dedicated to making a contribution to the freedom and happiness of your fellow humans. How is it, then, that there are millions of people out there in China, even in your native Southland, who are suffering worse than you are, and yet now that ME is in*

45

trouble, all you can think about is ME?

Immediately, this new standpoint changed my ability to judge. I realized that what my accusers were saying was not true, that the unjust treatment I was suffering could not be tolerated for long. If I could keep my health (physical and mental), I could wait out my captors and, one day, regain my freedom. Viewing things from the standpoint of "Big Me"—me as a conscientious member of the human race, not little, narrow selfish me—became essential for distinguishing truth from error. A subjective perspective is the enemy of objective truth.

Years prior to my incarceration, in my late teens, I organized youth social clubs among Alabama coal miners and steel workers. Wages in the South were much lower than in the North. Corporations could get away with this inequity because wages for Southern black workers were even lower. Employers divided the workers so they couldn't stand up together for their rights. They told the white workers, "You may be underpaid, but you're white like us, and you're way better than them."

In the beginning, you couldn't get a young white worker to sit down and eat with a black one. But once they started meeting together, discussing their common problems, getting a better understanding of each other, the racial tension cracked and broke very fast. Before long the workers were eating and drinking together with a particular pride, because they had established a new tradition and discarded the old habits that divided and damaged them all. Big Me had replaced little me in an important dimension.

I thought back over all the errors of judgment I had made over the years, and I realized that every one resulted from the interference of narrow selfishness, fear, bias, prejudice, groundless presuppositions, or blind faith in authority. We are born with adequate equipment for examining evidence and drawing logical conclusions. Narrow selfishness, bias, and blind faith may interfere with our native judgment so we make mistakes, but we can learn from our errors, improve our judgment, and grow wiser and more successful in the process.

Narrow selfishness is an important phrase. As John Donne wrote, "No man is an island, entire of itself." The wise person understands that his or her best interests can be served only when the best interests of others are also fulfilled. To protect one's personal interests, one needs to join with neighbors to preserve the peace, to overcome prejudice, to enforce reasonable tax laws, to assert constitutional liberties, and fulfill their obligations.

47

Lesson 9

TRAIN THE WILL

Each of the challenges I have described was a test of will. Will is the enforcer that pushes us to align our thoughts, emotions, and actions with the pursuit of our purpose. In some ways, will is like a muscle: exercise it and it strengthens; neglect it, and it grows flabby. Your will gradually strengthens through an accumulation of many little tests in which you successfully assert your will to enforce your purpose.

Look back at your own life story, and you will find incidents in which you asserted your will—made up your mind and succeeded in overcoming some difficulty to move forward. At other times when you tried to assert your will, the negative pulls and pressures were too strong, and you failed. But when you succeeded, your will was strengthened. You need to build on that.

My will was tested early on in 1941 during a strike in Birmingham, Alabama. Twenty years old, I was helping on the picket line—in fact, I was blocking the entrance way together with an elderly stenographer lady, wielding a black umbrella. In fact, we were the entire picket line.

Suddenly, a man-mountain of a strikebreaker, with a pistol in his right hand, threatened me. I was a small, skinny kid. My life was in danger and I was terrified. *Why the gun?* I thought. *He could squash me with one blow.* But I told myself that if I turned and ran, the workers I was supposed to be supporting would hold me in contempt, and I wouldn't be able to look at myself in the mirror when I shaved. So, frightened as I was, I stood my ground. And the workers drove the big goon off just before he got to me. That was a lesson for me: No matter how frightened you are, will yourself to do what you ought. Once you make up your mind, it makes whatever you have to do much easier.

I had plenty of opportunities to train my will during my incarceration. For example, in the prison, during the Cultural Revolution madness, when Mao was like a god and his Party press was unassailable, I saw something in the *People's Daily* about Mao's United States-sponsored peace negotiations with Chiang Kai-shek in 1945. I knew from my own experience that the article contained factual errors. I wanted to point this out and urge that it be corrected, but who was I to challenge the official press? A suspected criminal, being held in isolation for refusing to confess. If I took issue with the Party paper, it could only lead to punishment. But I felt, in good conscience,

I couldn't let this go. So I wrote my opinion on a piece of paper and handed it to the guard.

I don't know what he did with my note. Nothing happened. But the effort was a small assertion of my will to stand up for what was right, one of the many little exercises that led to a gradual strengthening of resolve.

On April 6, 1976, I was suddenly taken to an interrogation room to face three elderly officials, obviously men in leading positions. On the previous day, huge demonstrations had filled Tiananmen Square when the oppressive regime of Mao's chief assistants, the "Gang of Four," cracked down on people who came out to mourn the passing of their beloved premier Zhou Enlai. Yet because the Gang could not make their hatred of Zhou Enlai public, the crowds seized the situation to turn public grief into an angry protest against the Gang's cruel dictatorship—and even the rule of Mao himself. Fearing the opposition, the Gang sent an army of thugs to suppress the demonstration.

The next day, the *People's Daily* carried a long front-page screed, celebrating the suppression and denouncing Deng Xiaoping as the man responsible for stirring up trouble. (Deng, who led China in opening to the outside world and carrying out basic reforms, had been a victim of the Cultural Revolution, but had been brought back by

Mao to help manage the government.)

The three elder officials standing before me in the interrogation room wanted to know how I felt after reading the newspaper report. I thought that it was probably a test of my attitude toward the Party, but I made up my mind to be honest. *I'll probably be punished, but this is a big deal, and I'm going to tell them what I really think.*

I thought the newspaper report was false. I didn't know what was really going on, but I was certain that Deng could not be guilty as charged. "Deng grew up in the army," I said. "He is of the army, bone and sinew. He couldn't possibly have pushed bad elements to attack the army men, as the newspaper charged." Moreover, I was indignant at the rude way the paper mentioned Zhou Enlai. I couldn't help bursting into tears as I spoke.

This was another test of will—the three elders broke into broad smiles, obviously liking what I had said. I was not punished but encouraged. I had taken a chance to uphold the truth, and I felt good about voicing my real opinions. In that little cell, I recited to myself, over and over, the words of old Polonius in *Hamlet*:

> *This above all: to thine own self be true,*
> *And it must follow, as the night the day,*
> *Thou canst not then be false to any man.*

Lesson 10

CHECK WHAT'S
REALLY GOING ON

My most severe test came from an old vicious problem—
the frightening panic attacks that had plagued me for two
and a half decades. For several years (1967–1973) during
the Cultural Revolution, radical Red Guard types in the
garrison troops were put in charge of the prison, while the
original prison managers were themselves incarcerated.
The new keepers cursed at and mistreated the prisoners
(but not me, perhaps because I was an American citizen)
and there were beatings and physical torture in addition
to the basic horror of solitary confinement.

No one who has not experienced solitary confinement
can imagine the immense pressure of aloneness that the
prisoner has to endure, all day every day, month after
month, year after year. The loneliness presses in on your
ears, your eyes, your breathing, your very soul. You are
there with your own threat of madness sitting right opposite you, and you know it's either you or him. That's why
you have to think, exercise, plan a positive life for every

day, move, step by step, toward the future, whenever it may come.

My little cell was about six paces long and three paces across. A high window with a metal grate over it was set opposite the heavy wooden door. There were two light bulbs, one large for day, one small for night, a seatless commode, and a cold-water washbasin. The bed, under the window, was a wooden door placed over two sawhorses that had been cut down to half-height so the guards could watch you in bed. No pillow, just a paper-thin mat and a cotton quilt. That was it.

One night, I lay awake listening to a female prisoner being cruelly beaten, not far from my cell. I could hear the sound of something thumping on human flesh and the screams of the victim, begging for mercy. Her tormentors shouted at her. "Talk! If you want us to stop, you must talk!"

Lying there, enraged and utterly helpless, I was seized by an outsized panic attack. I felt as though the four walls of my cell were closing in to crush me, while the ceiling came down to meet the floor. It felt as if an iron hoop was tight across my forehead, pressing in, as my heart raced and I broke out in a cold sweat. There was no escape. Prisoners were not allowed to get up during the night, except to use the commode. I couldn't work off some of the tension by pacing up and down in my little cell. I just had to lie there and suffer.

Out of the desperation, a voice of reason spoke in my head: *Look at what is actually going on. Your pulse is fast, you're sweating, your nerves are tightening the skin on your forehead—and you're terrified that IT* (the horrifying breakdown during my first year in prison) *is going to come back and get you. That's all! You're just scared of IT. There isn't any IT! It's only your fear, added to those minor symptoms. There's nothing to be afraid of.*

Poof! The panic attack was gone, never to return. Never. I thought to myself, *What a triumph for reason and will!* It strengthened my confidence in being able to hold out, to keep learning, to prepare for the day of liberation.

When you have to face some horror, real or imagined, force yourself to check what the actual situation is—what's really going on, as opposed to what your frightened, often exaggerating mind tells you. A sober reality check will often cut the horror down to size and show you how to deal with it successfully.

Scholars like the distinguished brain scientist Antonio Damasio have shown that the thinking centers of our brain are hardwired to the seats of feeling and emotion.

At any given moment, our thinking is dominated by either the thought centers or the emotion centers, and a "switch" shifts our mind from thought-dominated to emotion-dominated judgments. It is important for us to learn how to "throw that switch" ourselves—to consciously subject our judgments to rational thinking, rather than let them be determined by blind emotion. That practice is a key to our clarity, to our actual freedom of choice and to our success.

Lesson 11

AVOID FIXATING ON
PERSONAL PROBLEMS

This was the issue that required the maximum exercise of will: What was I to do about the piercing love I felt for my wonderful Yulin and our four children? Our son had been only two when I was taken away: I worried he would have no memory of a father. Even sadder was the thought that I would forever miss seeing him and his sisters grow up.

I quickly understood one thing: If I allowed myself to fixate on missing Yulin and the family, then "that way madness lies." (Strange, how Shakespeare kept giving me lines at key moments!) Somehow, I had to put those thoughts out of my mind so that I could focus on the severe struggle facing me. I knew that Yulin would want me to do that. But one worry wouldn't go away: knowing her direct, upright ways, I was afraid that she would respond so harshly to her interrogators that she wouldn't survive. This anxiety was constantly present, but I had to learn to not let it overwhelm me. I remembered what Yulin told me as I was leaving our home for prison: "Keep a cool head. No wild talk." For her sake, I could not let myself break down or sink into depression because of worrying about her.

Real love derives joy from giving the other person joy. I had to not fixate on Yulin in order to show my true love for her. When I would be suddenly flooded with anxiety about her, I would shift my mind to how I could behave in the prison struggle so as to be worthy of her.

Lesson 12

CREATE YOUR
OWN FREEDOM

What is freedom? Could there be any freedom for me,
locked up in a space hardly big enough to park a car?
I thought of a man who has the legal right to cross a big
river. He should be free to do so. But is he? Only if he
is a swimmer, or if he can find a boat or a bridge, or a
ford through which he can wade. He should also know
something about the currents, the danger of alligators and
poisonous snakes. In other words, genuine freedom to
cross the river depends on a certain amount of knowledge.
Without that knowledge, his legal freedom means nothing.
Freedom is the understanding of necessity, said Hegel,
following on Spinoza. *Necessity* means the laws by which
things operate. Knowing the way things work gives you
the ability to deal with them—the freedom to work with
them and through them to achieve your purpose.

Understanding the way things worked in China and
in that prison, finding the study method that produced

58

results for me, and discovering ways of keeping up my health was knowledge that gave me a certain amount of freedom, even in captivity. So freedom, in the deeper sense, doesn't mean disregarding rules. Quite the opposite, it requires knowing the rules and how to use them to achieve one's purpose. As many have said, "Freedom isn't free."

Five

....

Applying Internal Insights to the Outside World

Whoever survives great calamity
will know great good fortune.
—Chinese Proverb

Curiously, the trials my wife, Yulin, and I both went through resulted in a happier, more productive, more stable life than we had ever imagined. Why? Because of what we were forced to learn to get through the hardships. Every hurdle that confronts us is both a challenge and an opportunity to learn something new to surmount the difficulties. Every negative turn of events has the potential to leave something new and good in its wake. Seeing the opportunity in a bad situation may not ease the suffering, but we must seize the chance to learn, to adjust, to grow, to benefit.

Take the sad example of a child who loses a beloved parent. A heavy blow, bringing a grief that cannot be denied. But the loss may force the child to learn greater independence, more versatile skills in dealing with life's problems, and so, even with the harm, the adversity may also lead to great good. I learned that it makes sense to try to convert every stumbling block into a stepping-stone. To see every challenge as an opportunity to learn how to move forward. That approach isn't overblown Pollyanna optimism—it's a process of struggle based on reality, not pious wishes, and an extremely important tool to use in dealing with whatever problems life hands us.

In March 1980, Yulin and I moved to America, literally without a penny. (There's some dispute over this: I remember that we actually had four pennies, but Yulin vigorously denies this, and she's usually right.) We had stopped taking all money from China—retirement pay, whatever. We hoped to consult for Americans going to China, and we didn't want to have conflict of interest issues by taking money from both sides. Besides, we wanted to leave what funds we had in Beijing for our four children, who were still there being watched over by a friend until we could bring them to join us. We had no experience in making a living in a capitalist country. Even the phrase, "making a living" was almost impossible to translate in the China of Mao Zedong, where the state was "Mama" who was expected to take care of everything. I was fifty-nine and Yulin was forty-eight. We were both moving toward retirement age. But we weren't retiring—we were just starting.

Well-meaning friends counseled us to go back to China, where we would be taken care of in comfort for life. But we prized our own freedom of expression and our commitment to furthering understanding between the United States and China. Not for a minute did we consider giving up and going back. We knew our disadvantages, but we tallied up our strengths. We had unparalleled experience, knowledge, and contacts in China. The Chinese market was drawing more and more attention from American businesses, but American executives had no idea who they were talking to when they went to China, where they had trouble even calling a taxi or ordering a meal, let alone successfully negotiating and implementing a deal.

Sooner or later, we knew, they would come knocking at our door. All we needed to do was to get along until that day came, and we would achieve our goals. While fulfilling our commitment, we would save enough money to retire without burdening our children, and create a safety net for anyone in the family who needed it. Most of all, we were confident in the strength of our love, certain that, sticking together as we always had, we would learn to deal with whatever came along.

How true all that proved to be!

My kinfolk and some old schoolmates filled in the gap until we became financially solvent. Through them, we benefited from the unbelievable kindness of strangers, people like artist Shirley Samberg of Roslyn, Long Island, who took care of our every need during the transition. Major media organizations were also supportive, and the government in Washington welcomed me home. Their help was like magic. Of course, we were in a special position, coming from persecution in China. But rest assured, there are good people who can come to your side when you need them—you are not really alone, although you may sometimes feel like it. The point is that if we hadn't recognized our own strengths and weaknesses, and based our life on using our advantages to overcome our disadvantages, none of our efforts would have been effective.

When big corporations finally did start asking for our services, at first we were anxious about our lack of experience in the business world: Could we really add value to their China operations? We did a reality check: What do they need from us? Not business skills—they have that already. What they needed was our help in bonding with people from a vastly different culture and help communicating clearly through the barriers of language and customs. Those tasks were something with which we were very familiar. With this analysis, we were emboldened to act as corporate consultants.

We applied what we learned about mind management to our consulting business. We were very clear about our purpose. Our aim was not to make ourselves rich or to have fun (although we did make money, and it was a great deal of fun!). Our goal was to promote mutually beneficial economic ties between America and China. We saw this goal as the most important of all the ties that bind different peoples together. That effort gave meaning to our lives.

In our consulting work, we laid down several principles (publicly announced) to ensure that we did not get involved in anything we considered dirty pool For example, we decided we would charge fixed consulting fees and would not accept commissions, finder's fees, success fees, or shares in revenue. Why? Because if your own income is involved in the client's success, and if you find out midstream that a deal is unethical or deceptive, you may be tempted to rationalize and go with it anyway. You don't have that problem if you get paid the same amount, win, lose, or draw.

We also decided that once we committed to a client project, we would do whatever was needed for its success. We were a mom-and-pop consultancy. If there was typing to be done, or files to be collated, or meetings to be set up, or accounts to be kept—we did it all. If we had to fly all night and negotiate all day, we did that. The clients knew they could depend on our best effort. As a result, we had almost no overhead, and clients paid our expenses for their own projects, so everything earned in consulting fees was pure gravy.

We were careful not to make extravagant promises to win a client. Once we were invited to a competitive bidding session with a major corporate executive, along with representatives from eleven other consultancies. Each consultant talked about the project's chance for success and how his or her assistance could guarantee it. We were the only ones who said plainly that mounting the project in China would be very difficult. We estimated the corporation had a 60 percent chance for success. We also said that we would focus on finding a good Chinese partner, who could share the client's vision, so that if the project didn't work they might be able, together, to shape an alternative that would work. Our consultancy was by far the smallest of all the contestants, but we won the bid—and the project ultimately succeeded, creating the first digital cell phone network in Shanghai.

Striving to base our business practices on clear cross-cultural communications, and sticking to the facts as we saw them gave us a thriving and successful business—and also allowed us to sleep well at night. The point is that our aim was to bring about the client's success, based on the facts. Our minds were relatively uncluttered by narrow selfish designs. This enabled us to follow that old Chinese saying: "seek truth from facts."

The key point about business, one too often forgotten, is that it is a relationship among people—not among goods or monies, but people. We tried to pick only clients who matched the values we had worked so hard to define and follow. Our best clients often became friends for life.

It may look easier to be crooked than to be honest, and more rewarding. But that is an illusion. We tell our clients, "He who goes to China for a quick kill gets quickly killed." Moreover, those who get rich by damaging others are seldom, if ever, happy with their wealth. We have known fabulously wealthy men who are seeing several different therapists each week, to try to find out why they are so unhappy.

Yulin and I often indulge in little "three minutes for self-appreciation" sessions, during which we look back with wonder and joy at the road we have traveled together and the openings ahead of us. Three minutes is plenty to just feel good about ourselves, but we spend much more time talking over our experience and the lessons learned. Our minds bring us two different types of signals: One represents illusion, the other, reality. Success and happiness depend largely on being able to distinguish between the two. It is not easy. In solitary, I'd frequently recite to myself a well-loved verse from the Bible: "Ye shall know the truth, and the truth shall set you free."

When Yulin and I moved to America, we found it somewhat confusing. It was a land in which more than half of marriages ended in divorce, more than half of the hospital beds were occupied by mental patients, more than half of underprivileged minority youth were unemployed, underemployed, or in jail. Big city streets were not safe at night. Many parks were combat zones. Those who could afford it tended increasingly to hunker down in gated communities, including us later on. What to think of this new home of ours?

We saw that America was still a growing, changing land, with a highly innovative people, most of whom wanted a fulfilling job, a happy family, a peaceful world. It was a country in which a young woman driver stopped her car at midnight in a pouring rain on a deserted street to ask two strangers (us) whether we needed help with our stalled auto.

Looked at objectively, America was still a land of opportunity—we exemplified that. But also one that faced outsized problems and serious challenges. We are convinced that the American people are gradually waking up, and that they will find ways to correct our whacked-out federal system. Those who are against progress and who get increasingly rich from the status quo would have us believe that the threat to America comes from China or Russia. We believe the real threat comes from our own troglodytes. But the days of their control are limited.

Six

....

Why Aren't You Bitter?

*"Harboring resentment is like drinking
poison and expecting someone else to die."*
—Anonymous saying

Since my return to America, "Why aren't you bitter?" is what
I get asked more than anything else. Often, I say, "What's so
great about being bitter? It only makes you unhappy."

Bitterness is painful, irritating, like a splinter in your heart.
It is usually fueled by resentment at some wrong someone
has committed against you. If you want to be at peace with
yourself, you need to eliminate it. And how do you do that?
Not, obviously, just by saying, "Go away! Leave me alone!"

When I was locked up in solitary there was a moment
every day when my gorge would rise and I would be gripped
by resentment. *How can they do this to me?* I would ask
myself. *It's so unjust!*

But then I would begin to analyze what made them do such things. My captors were part of a revolutionary movement, aimed at relieving hundreds of millions of people from crushing poverty and a life expectancy less than half that of industrialized countries. They had inherited a legal system designed to protect only the regime, not individuals. I was an unknown American, from a hostile country. I had won their complete confidence and was close to their top leaders. When I was accused of being a spy by their ally, the USSR, how could they not suspect me?

They were wrong about me, but they were right about liberating China. We were still on the same side, even if they didn't know it. With that perspective, all bitterness vanished and I resigned myself to their interrogations. So that's one way of getting rid of bitterness: finding the rationale behind the harm.

I forgave my captors for what they were doing to me.

But not all wrongs are forgivable, not by a long shot.

I used to think that forgiveness and eliminating bitterness were the same. But they are not. Eliminating the bitterness someone's actions cause you is about understanding that the actions are already in the past, that continued anger only hurts you, not the guilty party, and that to a certain extent the bitterness represents a continued hold that person has over you. It is his continued presence in your heart, where he does not belong. Relinquishing bitterness may have nothing to do with forgiveness. You are simply giving yourself permission to be free from the pain that the original wrongdoing produced.

"But they make me bitter by their wrongdoing," some people protest.

Wrong! You make yourself bitter because of your response to their offense. I once knew a six-year-old boy who used to demand toys, candy, and stuff from his father, and when he didn't get them, he would burst out crying. Then he would accuse his father, through the tears, "See, you made me cry again!" But who really made him cry? It was his own interpretation of his father's actions and his decision on how to respond that "made him cry."

The stimulus comes from outside, but the response, to a large extent, is up to us. If we decide that bitterness is a plague, we can think our way out of it. Indignation and resentment are useful only insofar as they may prompt effective action to remove harm. Otherwise, they simply fester inside us, elevate our blood pressure, disturb our rest. We must not allow the wrongdoers to maintain such a hold over us. When we manage our minds, we free ourselves of pain and seize the power we all have within us.

73

Made in the USA
Lexington, KY
20 October 2017